The Let's Talk Library ™

Let's Talk About Having Asthma

Elizabeth Weitzman

The Rosen Publishing Group's
PowerKids Press ™
New York

Published in 1997 by The Rosen Publishing Group, Inc.
29 East 21st Street, New York, NY 10010

First Edition

Book Design: Erin McKenna

Photo Illustrations: All photo illustrations by Carrie Ann Grippo.

Weitzman, Elizabeth
    Let's talk about when you have asthma / Elizabeth Weitzman.
        p.   cm. — (The Let's talk library)
    Includes index.
    Summary: Explains what asthma is, what causes it, and what sufferers can do to combat it.
    ISBN 0-8239-5032-8
    1. Asthma—Juvenile literature. 2. Asthma in children—Juvenile literature. [1. Asthma. 2. Diseases.]
I. Title. II. Series.
RC591.W386 1996
618.92'238—DC20
                                            96-27202
                                           CIP
                                         AC

Manufactured in the United States of America

Table of Contents

Jonah

After he scored a goal in the soccer game, Jonah had to stop playing. All of a sudden, he couldn't breathe. Then he started coughing, which made breathing even harder. His coach came running over. "Jonah? Are you okay?"

Jonah had been playing soccer for three years. Sometimes he coughed a lot when he ran too fast, but it was never this bad. He was scared. What was wrong with him?

◀ It's scary when it's hard to breathe.

What Is Asthma?

Like thousands of other kids and grown-ups, Jonah has **asthma** (AZ-muh). When he ran too hard and too fast during his soccer game, he had an **asthma attack** (AZ-muh uh-TAK). When someone has asthma, his or her **lungs** (LUNGZ) don't always work as well as other people's. Our lungs are what help us breathe. We breathe all the time without thinking about it. But if you have asthma, your lungs can sometimes make it harder for you to breathe.

Your lungs are working even when you don't realize it. ▶

Who Gets Asthma?

Anybody can have asthma. Usually, more than one person in a family has it. Just because someone in your family has asthma doesn't mean that you'll get it. But if you do have asthma, chances are someone else in your family does too.

People who have asthma often have **allergies** (AL-er-jeez) as well. This means that they have a bad **reaction** (ree-AK-shun) to certain things, such as dust or pets.

◀ People who have asthma often have allergies too.

When You Have Asthma

Most of the time, you probably won't even notice that you have asthma. But sometimes you may have asthma attacks. These may be caused by a bad reaction to a food you're **allergic** (uh-LER-jik) to. They may also be caused by exercising too hard. During an attack, you may feel like you can't breathe. To stop this, you may try to breathe harder or faster. This will make you feel weak or dizzy. You may not be able to stop coughing. And your chest may hurt.

Try not to be scared if you have an asthma ▶
attack. Take slow, deep breaths instead.

Having an Asthma Attack

Having an asthma attack can be very scary. But the best thing you can do is try to relax. It's hard to be calm when you're scared and don't feel well. But staying calm will help you begin breathing easier. It will also make you better able to remember to take your **medicine** (MED-ih-sin).

Find a grown-up to help you when you have an asthma attack. Your mom, dad, teacher, or coach will stay with you until you can breathe easier.

◀ A grown-up can help you with your asthma medicine.

13

Asthma Medicine

Most people with asthma have to take medicine. Some people take pills every day. Many others use an **inhaler** (in-HAY-ler) whenever they have an attack. An inhaler is a small metal can filled with medicine. It has a plastic tube that you use to breathe in the medicine.

Before you start using any medicine, you have to visit your doctor. She'll check to see if you have asthma. Then she'll tell you what medicine to take. She'll also show you the right way to use the inhaler if you need it.

Your doctor will answer any questions ▶
you have about your asthma.

When Medicine Is Not Enough

Taking your medicine when you're supposed to is very important. But there may be times when the medicine is not enough to make you better. If this happens, you may have to go to the **hospital** (HOS-pih-tul).

Although it may seem scary, a stay in the hospital will help you feel well again. The doctors there will be able to stop your asthma attack.

◀ Taking your medicine may keep you from having asthma attacks.

What Can You Do?

There are ways to keep some asthma attacks from happening. If you're allergic to certain things, like dogs, flowers, or chocolate, you should stay away from them. It may be hard at first, but you shouldn't cheat. Even a taste of peanut butter could make you sick if you're allergic to peanuts.

For some people, heavy exercise causes attacks. If you're one of those people, you may want to play sports that don't include a lot of running.

It's a good idea to stay away from the things you're allergic to. ▶

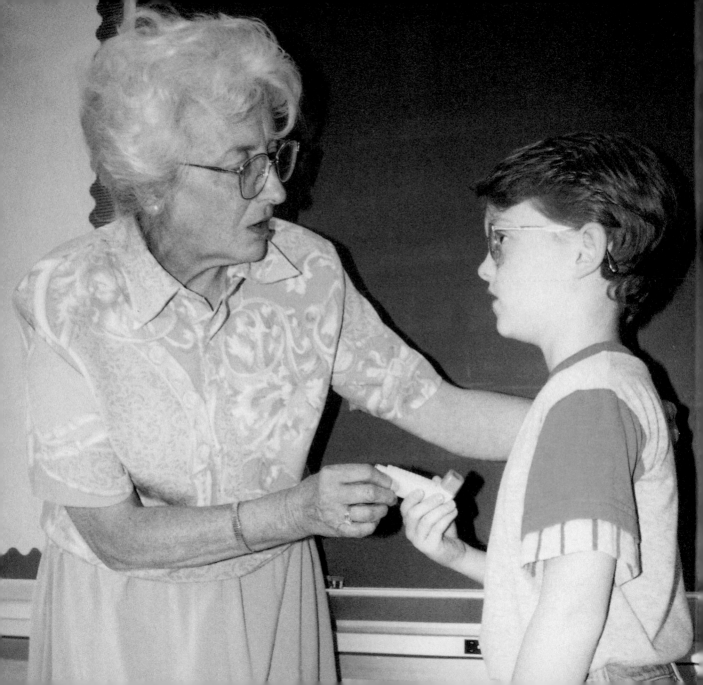

School

If you have asthma, you and your parents should let your teachers know. You can show them your inhaler and explain when you'll have to use it. It's a good idea to give them your doctor's phone number in case you ever need more help than your inhaler can give you. Tell them if certain exercises or sports make your asthma worse. They should also know if you're allergic to anything.

◀ Tell your teacher about your asthma. She can help you if you ever have an asthma attack at school.

Everybody's Different

Remember that everybody has something that makes them different. Some kids need to wear glasses. Others have to use inhalers.

In time, you'll learn what to avoid and when you need your medicine. Once you know how to control your asthma, you'll feel a lot better. And even if you do have an attack, you'll know how to help yourself.

Glossary

allergic (uh-LER-jik) Having a bad reaction to something that is usually harmless.

allergy (AL-er-jee) A bad reaction to a usually harmless thing.

asthma (AZ-muh) An illness that makes it hard to breathe sometimes.

asthma attack (AZ-muh uh-TAK) A time when asthma makes it hard for you to breathe.

hospital (HOS-pih-tul) Place for the care of the sick or hurt.

inhaler (in-HAY-ler) A small can filled with medicine that you breathe into your lungs.

lung (LUNG) One of two organs in a person's chest that help him breathe air.

medicine (MED-ih-sin) A chemical that helps your body.

reaction (ree-AK-shun) A response to something.

Index